I0480217

boss

['bäs, 'bȯs] *noun*

One who prides themselves in being Built On Self Success

TABLE OF CONTENTS

Built

Just 5 short years ago, my life seemed as if it were built on success. At the mark of 2012, I was graduating with honors from the top ranked HBCU in the nation. My credit score was LIT & life as a budding natural-ista was on the up-and-up! I landed my first full-time 'adulting' gig and soon after, I quickly began house hunting. I was a true millennial woman on the move!

Fast forward to 2016, where life led me to a different crossroads. Everything I did or felt suddenly became filtered through the struggle bus seat I was now currently occupying! Relationships became strained or severed altogether, my self-confidence plummeted to an all-time low and I had NO clue what my next move would be. For the first time   in forever, I had no idea what to do in any aspect of my life and it took a tremendous toll on me mentally, physically, most of all - spiritually. I im-mediately felt struck with the pressure to juggle a self-manufactured sense of success. I drove myself INSANE by stretching myself thin; I got to do what I truly loved in the 5-to-9 stretch, so long as I could fit it within my comfort zone of a 9-to-5 lifestyle.

One early Sunday morning, a quiet, sure voice in my Spirit finally spoke up and said: "You've done it your way for long enough! NOW is time to stand firm on the foundation that is true in your heart - TRUST ME." That next morning, I went to work and submitted my two weeks notice, still unsure of what would happen thereafter.

Maybe you are also in a season where you're facing your own giant decisions. Whether it's an investment into a partnership, new career or school, major financial decision - WHATEVER! - I learned RULE # 1 is...there's no one else BUILT for this life, these experiences and this jour-ney but you! We invite you to spend this first week preparing to open your heart and mind to who you truly are. Let's get a blueprint mapped out to build something great together!

- QUEEN ASH

(BUILT On Self Success)

DAY 1

B.O.S.S. THOUGHTS

The first letter in B.O.S.S represents BUILT. Use the space below to build
a list of as many B-words you can think of that describe you best!

(i.e. Boss, Bold, Beautiful, and so on!)

DAY 2

THE FOUNDATION OF THE THRONE

#theTRUTH

"For no one can lay any foundation other than the one
already laid, which is Jesus Christ."

— 1 Corinthians 3:11

#thePOINT

Are you a BOSS or a BITCH? Women are constantly subjected to all kinds of labels...most of which are associated with negative, degrading connotations. What matters first and foremost is what you believe about yourself! Think back on the list of B-words from the previous day. Are these words you chose helping build the framework of the life you live?

#theTAKEAWAY

"If you have built castles in the air, your work need not be lost; that is where they should be. Now put the foundations under them."

— Henry David Thoreau

#BOSSBONUS

THANK YOU GOD for giving me the foundation to build a life of honor and legacy. I will remain faithful no matter what season I'm in; because I know I can come to Your Throne for anything I need. I want to be a woman of excellence and a reflection of your goodness! Use this time to show me any areas of my life where you want me to grow and flourish. AMEN!

DAY 3

PURSUING PURPOSE

#theTRUTH

> "We love because He first loved us."
>
> — 1John4:19

#thePOINT

I was having a conversation with a friend as graduation was approaching; when he gave me a simple, yet profound piece of advice. His affirmation still rings in my head to this day, "GROWTH IS EVERYTHING. GOD IS EVERYTHING ELSE!" This is one of many mantras I use as a catalyst for pursuing the passions that light a fire within my soul. Following God's will for your life (not anyone else's) will always lead you in the right direction.

#theTAKEAWAY

> "Living with purpose means wisely choosing and committing to a few of the best things for the season of life you're in."
>
> — Crystal Paine

#BOSSBONUS

Remember that game plan we discussed? Start today by taking an evaluation of where you are now! What are your strengths? What about weaknesses? Are there any opportunities available, or at least any that you can start on your own? What threats could potentially slow or stop you from moving ahead? On a separate sheet, break down each of these quadrants in a SWOT analysis.

What is S.W.O.T? *Strength/Weakness/Opportunities/Threats*

DAY 4

WATCH THE THRONE

#the**TRUTH**

"This calls for patient endurance on the part of the people of God who keep His commands and remain faithful to Jesus."

— Revelation 14:12

#the**POINT**

Rome wasn't built in a day, and neither will you! It takes time, patience and endurance to carry the crown of mastering your heart's desires. What you work towards will produce the right fruit; should you make the decision to yield the labors of your work to sacrifice, in exchange for an excellent reputation.

#the**TAKEAWAY**

"The goal isn't to live forever, the goal is to create something that will."

— Chuck Palaniuk

#BOSSBONUS

Take out the SWOT analysis you did the day before. Use the quadrants to identify 3 goals you want to focus on (personal, professional, purposeful: one of each) For each goal, create a SMART plan! See the next page for how to layout your own SMART goals.

S.M.A.R.T. GOALS

S - SPECIFIC (SIMPLE, SENSIBLE, SIGNIFICANT)

ANSWER THE WHO, WHAT, WHEN, WHERE, WHY + HOW OF YOUR GOAL!

M - MEASURABLE (MEANINGFUL + MOTIVATIONAL)

HOW WILL YOU KNOW WHEN YOU'VE ACHIEVED YOUR GOAL?

A - ACHIEVABLE (ATTAINABLE)

IS THE GOAL YOU'VE SET TO ACHIEVE FOR YOURSELF REALISTIC?

R - RELEVANT (RESOURCED + RESULTS-BASED)

HOW DOES THIS IMPACT YOUR BUSINESS MISSION, VISION, OR VALUES?

T - TIME BOUND (TIME + COST SENSITIVE)

WHAT'S THE DEADLINE?

ROYAL SOURCE: www.mindtools.com/pages/article/smart-goals.htm

DAY 5

WATCH THE THRONE

#the TRUTH

"Yahweh answered me, "Write the vision, and make it plain on tablets, that he who runs may read it."

— Habakkuk 2:2

#the POINT

Having a Mission Vision and Values statements - or MVVs - that you live by will serve as a guiding light on your B.O.S.$. journey. In order to set yourself on a sure foundation, it's important to know what matters most to you. When you know who you are and what you stand for, it makes it easier to be decisive when making decisions on if an opportunity will be a good fit for you!

#the TAKEAWAY

"The only thing worse than being blind is having sight and no vision."

— Hellen Keller

#BOSSBONUS

Make it your mission to have a mission statement! What's most important to you? What do you value in life? How do you want your name to be remembered? Share these thoughts with another QUEEN close to you today.

DAY 6

QUEENIN' AIN'T EASY!

#theTRUTH

"But you are a chosen people, a royal priesthood, a holy nation, God's special possession, that you may declare the praises of Him who called you out of darkness into His wonderful light."

— 1Peter2:9

#thePOINT

No one ever said the keys to the kingdom would come easy; they only promised it will be worth it! Stop thinking because your progress isn't matching up with someone else's that you aren't taking ground. This is why a foundation FIRST is so important! Be vigilant and detailed along the way; but leave some breathing room to always grow from your mistakes.

#theTAKEAWAY

"You are not born with a fixed amount of resilience. Like a muscle, you can build it up, draw on it when you need it. In that process, you will figure out who you really are—and you just might become the very best version of yourself."

— Sheryl Sandberg

#BOSSBONUS

THANK YOU GOD for your promises given to me as the daughter of a King. I want to pursue the BEST you have to give, and I understand that starts with mapping out a game plan. I pray I will continue to learn and grow into the Queen I am destined to be as my relationship with you continues to build. AMEN!

DAY 7

<u>B.O.S.$. THOUGHTS</u>

Reflect on what you've learned in this first week. Use the space below
to begin mapping out your next five year plan. Where do you see
yourself, both personally or professionally?
Be as detailed as possible; write it out - make it clear!

O<small>N</small>

About a year and a half ago, I was literally in a whole different state; 7 hours away from my friends and family at a job I literally hated. On top of that, relationship issues were draining my energy and focus – it was all too much!

Everyday I'd literally get off work, come home to my apartment, turn the TV on mute and just lay on my couch - in silence - not wanting to really speak to anyone about anything. I just wanted God to put all the answers in front of me, without much work being done on my behalf. I mean after all, I was tired from working 10 hour days.

That all changed in May 2016. Three months before my lease was up, I decided that to be where I wanted to be in life I'd have to make things happen on my own. I realized I'd have to take the first steps myself and then God would handle the rest! I had to make sure I was ON it, if I wanted to move back home.

I began by buckling down and taking some kind of step everyday towards my goals of relocating and truly being happy. I was at work in-between calls filling out applications. When I came home, I utilized that time to research photography, music, art, blogging, branding - all the things that truly made me happy! In early July, I had a job waiting for me back home. By mid-August, I sold almost EVERYTHING I had, packed as much stuff that could fit in my car and headed up the interstate. The point is this: ANY and EVERYTHING YOU WANT TO DO, CAN BE DONE - BUT IT WILL NOT JUST FALL IN YOUR LAP! You've got to make time to be ON it, whether you're tired or not! Whatever it is in life, if you want it, YOU'VE got to take it ON full force...every second of everyday!

- **QUEEN ASIA**

(Built **ON** Self Success)

DAY 8

B.O.S.$. THOUGHTS

The O in B.O.S.S represents ON. What's that thing that's constantly cap-
tivating your time and attention the most? Name any areas you feel
you need to focus ON during this next week!

DAY 9

NEVER LET YOUR CROWN TILT

#the**TRUTH**

"Delight yourself in the Lord,
and He will give you the desires of your heart."

— Psalm 37:9

#the**POINT**

Going through life, in the search of finding yourself or walking into your purpose, you must know that it will NOT all be pixie dust and glitter! Some days will be more gritty than others. There will be days in which you feel you have it 'all figured it out'; There will also be times where you'll want to throw in the towel to quit! Either way it goes, understand that you must make sure you keep confidence, dignity and pride in your journey. Don't give up and don't get discouraged when it's looking tough. Adjust your crown - then dig in deeper! You are closer to the surface than you actually think!

#the**TAKEAWAY**

"The secret to change is to focus all of your energy, not on fighting the old but on building the new"

— Socrates

#BOSSBONUS

List your short term goals for the week as they pertain to your life, job/school, passion, etc.

DAY 10

KEEP THE CROWN POLISHED

#the TRUTH

"Be still before the Lord, and wait patiently for Him"

— Psalm 37:7

#the POINT

You must always understand that in the process of being on top of things, you will have periods of doubt or question - and that is perfectly natural. There is nothing you cannot do as long as you continue to keep the faith in your purpose! Never cease in realizing that you are gifted, talented and great beyond measure! There may be doors of opportunity that may not open for you just yet, simply because there may be a better door God has for you. Either way don't let ANY obstacles or setbacks deter you on your way to the top!

#the TAKEAWAY

"The key is not to prioritize what's on your schedule but to schedule your priorities"

— Stephen Covey

#BOSSBONUS

Name one obstacle you've overcome that you thought you wouldn't. Now list two things that the situation taught you about yourself.

DAY II

EVERY CROWN IS UNIQUE

#theTRUTH

"God is the only one who can make the valley of
trouble a door of hope"

— Hosea 2:15

#thePOINT

We're living in a world that is so pressed on instant gratification. It can be easy to find yourself comparing your race to the success of others. Well, let us stop you right there! Everything you've done so far - all the effort put into YOUR race - is done for a reason. You can not compare yourself - or your success - to that of others. You never know what the next person had to do to get where they are! Everyone's story is different and unique in its own way. Focus all your energies and efforts on you and your progress and you'll be just fine.

#theTAKEAWAY

"It's not about perfect. It's about effort. And when you bring that effort
every single day, that's where transformation happens.
That's how change occurs"

— Jillian Michales

#BOSSBONUS

Challenge yourself to clear your mind of clutter today. Fast from social media and music until the morning and channel your focus on inner peace.

DAY 12

HEAVY IS THE HEAD THAT WEARS THE CROWN

#theTRUTH

"My help comes from the Lord, the Maker of heaven and earth"
— Psalm 121:2

#thePOINT

You're filled with brilliant ideas and you can do it all! You know that feeling you had about the one business idea you came up with? DO IT. Kick doubt to the curb and just go for it! How will you ever know what it could have done for you if you don't try? No one said it would be easy - but what in life is!? Try it and if it works perfect - if it doesn't, at least there are a million things you can now take away as a learning experience from what was done. Allow this to advance you and also help you skip over similar things that may come back around in future obstacles or other plans later in life. Either way it's bound to be a win-win!

#theTAKEAWAY

"When you want to succeed as bad as you want to breathe then you'll be successful"
— Eric Thomas

#BOSSBONUS

Take 30 minutes of your day today to do something toward your business brand or goal 30 minutes when you wake up this morning and 30 minutes before bed.

DAY 13

CROWN YOURSELF QUEEN

#theTRUTH

"Let us not grow weary of doing good, for in due season,
we will reap if we do not give up"

— Galatians 6:9

#thePOINT

"Slow and steady wins the race..." I'm sure we've all heard this one; but do we actually take heed to the meaning behind the quote is the question. Consistency is key in all things that you do towards your success. But do we also understand that it may be a little slow getting to reap the benefits of our work, EVEN IF you're the best at what you do! You will run into times where it seems as if things just aren't moving fast enough for you; but ask yourself this: Would you rather rush into something temporary or pace yourself to develop something of longevity and sustainability?

#theTAKEAWAY

"It does not matter how slowly you go as long as you do not stop."

— Confucius

#BOSSBONUS

Compose a one-year plan of where you would ideally like to be in life as it pertains to your business, brand and personal goals! Draw it out on a timeline and be as detailed as possible!

DAY 14

B.O.S.$. THOUGHTS

Review the previous week's activities. Name some NEW areas you need to focus ON during this next upcoming week to keep momentum up!

Self

In 2016, I fell into a dark stage in my life. I became overwhelmed with obstacles, which in turn caused me to shut down mentally and emotionally. I went through the motions of life daily; battling the demons I faced internally. I felt alone, misunderstood and ironically, scared. I feared what would happen if I didn't find a way to get help to better my mind, body and spirit. I was unsure of how to climb out of this deep hole of feeling pity, sorrowful and defeated.

Eventually I realized the issue wasn't the adversities I was facing at all - but rather my mindset. I was only focused on the negative potential outcomes of everything I was experiencing at the time. Here I was, feeling as if I had allowed my beauty, intelligence and talent to go to waste. After a conversation with a friend who questioned why I viewed life with a "half empty" mindset, she reminded me of the power of prayer. I realized I had been looking at the glass half empty for so long that I neglected to see the fact that God has blessed me with so much! That friend helped to remind me that at the age of 21, I have accomplished an abundance of things. I have graduated with honors from an esteemed University in four years. During my junior year, I launched my company - Jalice & Co. As a leader, mentor, and female activist - among other things - I represent a prime example of BLACK EXCELLENCE! I am beautiful, I am intelligent and most of all - I AM HUMAN!

As I began to get back into my readings, devotions, exercising and healthy eating habits - day by day I noticed the growing improvements inside and out. Have you ever heard of the phrase "you are what you eat"? Well likewise, YOU ARE WHAT YOU THINK! Over the next week we will work on building a healthier you, inside and out! Breaking down the importance of SELF LOVE and bringing you one step closer to being BUILT ON SELF SUCCESS!

XOXO,

QUEEN NAJEE

(Built On **SELF** Success)

DAY 15

B.O.S.$. THOUGHTS

The first S in B.O.S.S stands for SELF. What is your definition of
self-love? Do you show yourself enough appreciation?

DAY 16

FLAWS AND ALL

#the TRUTH

"And let endurance have its perfect effect so that you will be perfect
and complete, not deficient in anything."

— James 1:4

#the POINT

It's perfectly alright to not be perfect because everything you
aren't makes you who you are, too! Today, we want you to come to
acknowledge those flaws and create a plan of action to work on bettering
them so they don't hinder your progress on the road to success. The key
is to first FACE those imperfections, then set in PLACE a plan of action
and ERASE anything that contributes to you not feeling beautiful or successful, inside and out #FACEPLACEERASE!

#the TAKEAWAY

"Without continual growth and progress, such words as improvement,
achievement, and success have no meaning."

— Benjamin Franklin

#BOSSBONUS

List three flaws you face externally, internally and professionally.

1.

2.

3.

Referring to the above list, think of a correlating action you can take daily to re-
verse those imperfections.

1.

2.

3.

DAY 17

WO(MAN) IN THE MIRROR

#theTRUTH

"To acquire wisdom is to love oneself; people who cherish understanding will prosper. "

— Proverbs 19:8

#thePOINT

Everything has beauty, but not everyone sees it, especially if it's within ourselves. Remind yourself often that you are worth it. Daily affirmations are a great way to set a positive mindset before starting your day. Take a few seconds to stand in front of the mirror and repeat after me:

"I am beautiful!" "I am intelligent!" "I am strong!" "I am courageous!" "I AM successful!" "I may not be perfect but I am worth it!" "I am a QUEEN!"

#theTAKEAWAY

"Love yourself first and everything else falls into line. You really have to love yourself to get anything done in this world."

— Lucille Ball

#BOSSBONUS

List five things that you love about yourself. What makes you, YOU?

1.
2.
3.
4.
5.

DAY 18

FACE YOUR FEARS

#the**TRUTH**

"The Lord is my light and my salvation—whom shall I fear? The Lord is the stronghold of my life—of whom shall I be afraid?"

— Psalm 21:1

#the**POINT**

Underneath your fears lie great opportunities. Your unique way of thinking is what tailors your destiny. It's common for most people to put 'caps' on their level of success because they fear what may lie ahead. Your fears will, in turn, overpower your thoughts and actions if you allow them to. You want the ugly truth? Failure, judgment, criticism, debt, lost friendships or broken relationships, lack of trust and disappointments can all - and most likely - will happen when you decide to embark on any journey in life. I'm here to tell you that IT IS OKAY! Don't allow these experiences to break you, learn from them and use them as tools to help make you successful!

#the**TAKEAWAY**

"Fears are nothing more than a state of mind."

— Napoleon Hill

#BOSSBONUS

Grab a sheet of paper and write a letter to yourself discussing any and all fears or worries you have in your life right now. Once you're done, tear the paper into tiny pieces, go stand outside and allow them to blow away. Repeat this activity every time you find yourself worrying and hindering your progress.

DAY 19

THE GREATEST WEALTH IS HEALTH

#theTRUTH

"...seek peace and pursue it"

— Psalm 34:14

#thePOINT

Many people neglect their physical, emotional and mental health to solely focus on the monetary gains they are seeking. When you do, your body pays the price for the lack of attention you give it. Part of the process of loving yourself is taking care of your body. Eating clean, exercising and meditating and venting to a trusted friend are just some of a few activities that can help get you to a better, healthier you. Start by making efforts to take the stairs instead of the elevator, consult a chef for meal prep ideas or end your day with a moment of reflection and prayer. The most ignored fact is that most people shy away from coming to terms with their mental health. Throughout our lives, we go through the motions of stressful situations without giving our brain a break or a chance to relieve itself before enduring more! Meditation or simply talking to someone trustworthy whether it's a friend or therapist is essential.

#theTAKEAWAY

"The groundwork for all happiness is good health"

— Leigh Hunt

#BOSSBONUS

Take a second to focus on your breath. Allow yourself to be still for one moment and simply breathe. Begin by breathing slowly in your nose and out of your mouth. Let your mind draw blank and wander into the distance, not thinking about any obligations or distractions letting all worries go. Reach a point of peace within you then continue to have a great day!

DAY 20

SPREAD LOVE, IT'S THE QUEEN WAY!

#theTRUTH

"My command is this: love each other as I have loved you. Greater love has no one than this: to lay down one's life for one's friends."

— John 15:12

#thePOINT

Spreading love is something this world needs a little more of! Pointing out the good in others helps us find the good in ourselves. Do you take notice of how you feel after volunteering or donating to a good cause? Why not have that feeling all of the time!? We don't always have to have a reason to give to those in need or find a way to brighten someone's day. Start by making a conscious effort to smile more. Energy is reciprocal, and the kind you give could affect those around you tremendously. Remember, it all starts with you!

#theTAKEAWAY

"Spread love everywhere you go. Let no one ever come to you without leaving happier"

— Mother Teresa

#BOSSBONUS

As you go through your day today, see how many of the following tasks you can accomplish:

Slip a nice note into someone's pocket	*Call someone distant and tell them you love them*
Give someone a high five	**Compliment someone**
Forgive someone who has done any wrong doing to you	*Spark a conversation with a stranger*
Pray with someone	**Smile at 10 people**

DAY 21

<u>B.O.S.$. THOUGHTS</u>

Take time to reflect on some of the topics we discussed this week.
Do you have a better understanding of the importance
and benefit of loving yourself?

Success

As a Queen, YOU are in control of your destiny! To the public eye, success is considered accomplished once you've reached a certain stature of popularity or by attaining large profits. It is embedded in many of us as children that we must conform to the idea of having an abundance of money or material things to be "happy". Well, they were wrong. The true meaning of success is to accomplish your goals or purpose - no matter how big or small.

Everyone loves a good "Rags to Riches" triumph but how about creating a #GLO'UP story of your own? No two paths will ever be the same when it comes to being successful, so do not allow the means of those around you to dictate and determine how far you can go. WE CAN support one another and stay focused on our unique vision while also paving your own journey. As a matter of fact, we want to start leading the change!

Pay off that debt, get that new car, build your dream home, launch the company you always envisioned...LIVE HAPPY. At the end of the day, that is all that matters! Genuine joy brings the satisfaction of knowing you are not in 'need' of anything. You can fulfill your wants, as desired. We hope that if you haven't already, you'll join our QUEENDOM movement - QUEENS in the City - to continue empowering, supporting and motivating others in royal courts just like yours!

As we embark on this final week, we hope you take time to truly reflect on the royal contents of this book. We hope these jewels you'll walk away with shine light on your own understanding of how to be Built On Self Success (BOS$)!

If you ever feel yourself losing focus or falling unmotivated, grab this BOSS tool kit and refresh yourself on WHY your crown sits so high. You are destined for greatness Queen, now it's up to you to go out there and TAKE IT!

#KEEPQUEENIN!

With Love,

QUEENS IN THE CITY

(Built On Self **SUCCESS**)

DAY 22

B.O.S.$. THOUGHTS

The last S in B.O.S.S. is our favorite: SUCCESS! Thinking back over the month, how would you now define success? Has your definition changed since you started?

DAY 23

HAVING A POSITIVE IMAGE

#theTRUTH

"Do not conform to the pattern of this world, but be transformed by
the renewing of your mind."

— Romans 12:2

#thePOINT

In our society today, your image means EVERYTHING! It defines
who you are, what you do, who you choose to associate yourself with
and most importantly who chooses to associate themselves with you! It's
important to ensure that you are keeping a clean and positive image,
both personally and professionally. Be mindful of the things you share,
especially on social media.

PRO TIP: *If you have to question whether or not it would be deemed
as appropriate, then the answer is NO!*

Also, be aware of how you carry yourself in public! Your choice of
words, clothing and behavior will be the first impression for a potential
business partner or client. What is the assumption you would want to be
made of yourself? No, you don't have to stop being yourself, just understand that there is a time and place for everything!

#theTAKEAWAY

"Elegance isn't solely defined by what you wear. It's how you carry
yourself, how you speak, what you read"

— Carolina Herrera

#BOSSBONUS

Take the time today to review and clean up your social media
pages, give away a few clothes that no longer fit you or your career goals
or think of ways to release some old habits that may affect your daily
glam routine.

PRO TIP: *As a professional, grooming is important. Keep your hair,
nails, hygiene and overall image taken care of!*

DAY 24

PRESSURE MAKES DIAMONDS

#theTRUTH

"Every good and perfect gift is from above"

— James 1:17

#thePOINT

People admire INDIVIDUALITY. Stepping outside 'the box' is perfectly normal. In fact, it's actually a great idea when it pertains to your brand or business! I mean think about it - don't you get tired of the same old marketing strategies? Exactly! Always be willing to step out on a leap of faith and try new things. Remember you'll never know how something will turn out in your favor until you try.

#theTAKEAWAY

"If you want to be the best you have to do things that other people aren't willing to do."

— Michael Phelps

#BOSSBONUS

What are three things you have been nervous about starting or trying? A new hairstyle? Idea proposal at work? Recipe?

1.

2.

3.

Tonight, cross one of those things off of the list and give it a shot!

DAY 25

TUNNEL VISION TO THE THRONE

#theTRUTH

"Perhaps this the moment for which you were created"

— Esther 4:14

#thePOINT

Have you ever second-guessed an Idea or plan you've had? Perhaps every now and again, you've put it on the back burner and left it there to marinate. But imagine 2 months down the line, that SAME idea you once had, someone else took off with it and made it into a business. I bet you'd feel some type of way, huh!? Your ideas are things that come to your mind for a reason! Act on them, pursue them - DON'T STOP - recognize what you want and put those dreams into fruition!

#theTAKEAWAY

"If you don't go after what you want, you'll never have it. If you don't ask the answer will always be no. If you don't step forward, you're always in the same place"

— Nora Roberts

#BOSSBONUS

Let's break this idea down a bit further to prepare for ACTION!!

What's your main Objective?

What's the guiding Purpose?

Who's your target Audience?

Are there potential Benefits?

What about Roadblocks?

DAY 26

JUST KEEP SWIMMING!

#theTRUTH

"I will not cause pain without allowing something new
to be born, says the Lord"

— Isaiah 66:9

#thePOINT

You can't be afraid to fail to obtain success! Yes, I said <u>FAIL</u>! Sometimes things will go wrong. Yes, unplanned circumstances do happen. Things can be disastrous at times but that's totally ok! As long as you understand that you should be prepared mentally for things to happen that are beyond your control, you'll be great at who and what you are.

#theTAKEAWAY

"Stop being afraid of what could go wrong, and start being
excited of what could go right"

— Tony Robbins

#BOSSBONUS

Have you ever seen Finding Nemo? In this film, one of the main characters - a loving, yet forgetful fish named Dory (played by Ellen DeGeneres) - taught us the importance of persevering no matter what gets in your way. As you "keep swimming" through life, know that it is OK to make mistakes. Learn from them and swim on, sis! Take a sheet of paper out today and list three or more lessons you've learned thus far and share them with a friend!

LEGENDARY: BE HUMBLE!

#the**TRUTH**

> "Teach me to do your will, for you are my God! Let your
> good Spirit lead me on level ground!"
>
> — Psalm 143:10

#the**POINT**

QUEENS who make history are often the ones that most people think are crazy for thinking they could ever do such a thing in the first place! Success is only going to come to those who aren't afraid to GET UP AND GO GET what they set their hearts   on! However, a legendary mentality requires insurmountable amounts of maturity! It is important to remain humble and keep your faith strong as you work for your dreams come to fruition.

#the**TAKEAWAY**

> "The people who are crazy enough to think they can change
> the world are the ones who do"
>
> — Steve Jobs

#BOSSBONUS

Who do you look up to whether it be in your industry or life, in general? Why do you admire them? Do you notice similar attributes in yourself?

1.

2.

3.

4.

5.

DAY 28

B.O.S.$. THOUGHTS

Ok, Queen! You now have what it takes to be Built On Self Success!
The only question left is, WHAT NEXT!? Take a look over your journey
throughout our time together in this book. How will you apply what
you've learned to bring your vision to life?

How will <u>YOU</u> become B.O.S.$.?